Henry Horenstein is the author of *Black and White Photography* and *Beyond Basic Photography*, both widely used texts, and co-author (with Brendan Boyd) of *Racing Days*. He teaches at Rhode Island School of Design.

Brendan Boyd is a syndicated columnist and co-author of *Racing Days*. He is also author of the award-winning *The Great American Baseball Card Book*.

Robert Garrett, a freelance writer, is a former editor for the *Boston Herald,* and writes regularly for *The Boston Globe*.

HOOPS

Behind
the Scenes
with the
Boston Celtics

HO

Behind the Scenes
with the Boston Celtics

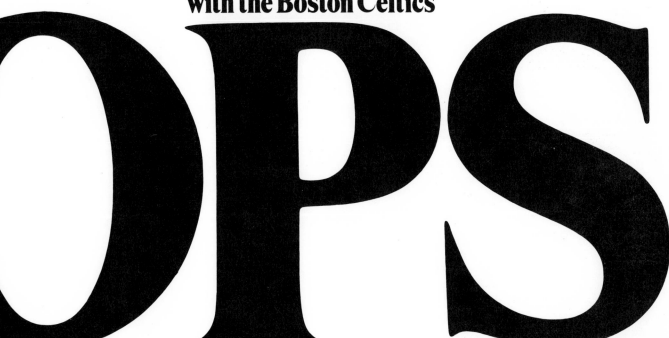

OPS

Photographs by
Henry Horenstein

Text by
Brendan Boyd
and Robert Garrett

Little, Brown & Company
Boston   Toronto   London

THIS BOOK IS FOR MARK, KAREN, AND SARAH,
A FUTURE HOOPSTER.

ACKNOWLEDGMENTS

Many thanks to the Boston Celtics organization, especially Jan Volk, for making *Hoops* happen. Special thanks also goes to Tod Rosensweig, Steve Lipofsky, and Jeff Twiss of the Celtics and Bill Marshall and Gary Way of NBA Properties. The following were generous with their time and we thank them too: Danny Ainge, Dan Dyrek, Chris Ford, Richard Garrett, Dennis Grabowski, Grant Gray, Jon Jennings, Dennis Johnson, K. C. Jones, Ed Lacerte, Wayne Lebeaux, Brad Lohaus, Mike Mundt, Joe Qatato, Steve Reagan, Jimmy Rodgers, Arnold Scheller, Vladimir Shulman, and David Zuccaro.

A POND PRESS BOOK

PRODUCTION: POND PRESS
ART DIRECTOR: BOB CIANO
ASSISTANT ART DIRECTOR: ROBIN MICHALS
EDITORIAL ASSOCIATE: LAUREN LANTOS
COPY EDITOR: TERI KEOUGH
DARKROOM TECHNICIAN: MIKE CAREY

FIRST EDITION
Library of Congress Catalog Card Number 88-82539
ISBN: 0-316-37319-2 hc
0-316-37309-5 pb

HC: 10   9   8   7   6   5   4   3   2   1
PB: 10   9   8   7   6   5   4   3   2   1

Published simultaneously in Canada by Little, Brown & Company (Canada) Limited
PRINTED IN THE UNITED STATES OF AMERICA

CONTENTS

A scorekeeper high above the court.

If heaven won't help the home team, cheering for them might.

The game heats up as Bird defends the basket.

Celtics president Red
Auerbach, deep in
concentration.

Larry Bird and Robert Parish in a rare relaxed moment during practice.

And now for our national anthem.

Foreword

Every sports team is a family. The pickup softball team is a family for an hour, the high-school football team a family for a year. The professional baseball team is a family until its franchise dissolves, or until its individual members are traded or retire.

Of all the major professional sports teams, however, the pro basketball team resembles a family most. That's partly because it has the fewest players. The smaller the team, the tighter the bond. But it's also because basketball is such a simple game. It

has the simplest goal—to throw a big ball through a slightly bigger hoop—has few rules, is played in a small space, and requires minimal equipment. Everything about the game is spare. So there is little to divert the players from the game itself or from their teammates—their need for them, their closeness to them.

To watch professional sports today is to be distracted by the complexity of it all—the mammoth arenas with computerized seating plans, the multi-year player contracts with complicated clauses, the

Dennis Johnson talks to a spectator at practice.

thick playbooks full of x's and o's. But to concentrate on the game itself, especially on the game of professional basketball, is to see how surprisingly simple it remains, how close to the schoolyard of childhood. Every pro basketball team still has twelve players and one head coach and a trainer with a training table and some tape. There's still one ball and two hoops and no way to get any better at playing than by practicing. And all the work necessary to win is still what brings the members of the family together—in uniform and out.

Jimmy Rodgers takes charge at practice.

This book is a behind-the-scenes look at the daily activities of one team, one family, of professional basketball players. It is not a history of the team, or an in-depth re-creation of one of its seasons, or an examination of the business workings of professional basketball. It is, rather, a series of snapshots of the members of one family—players, coaches, equipment managers, ball boys, scouts—and a glimpse at the routines that enable that family to play the game as well as they can.

It's a family album.

K. C. Jones can't play for his team, but he can watch and worry.

Celtics

The Boston Celtics have always taken the family concept of team play much further than most sports organizations.

They've had seven coaches since 1965, and all but two played for the team. Three of their four current scouts are ex-Celtics, as are both the TV colormen. Former players call Celtics president Red Auerbach for personal and career advice. Ex-Celtics hang around during practice, shooting baskets and chatting with the guys. It's like a perpetual family reunion. Pride in winning and joy in the tradition are the constants.

This tradition is something Auerbach nurtures carefully. He is the father of the family, having served as Celtics coach, general manager, or president for thirty-eight years. He believes in loyalty—of player to team, and of team to player. Any player who puts himself above the team is bounced quickly, regardless of talent.

The Celtics also like to promote from within. Jan Volk, the current general manager, began at Auerbach's summer camp as a teenaged assistant. Every

It's only a short walk from the locker room to the court.

Celtics employee, from the office receptionist Linda Hobbs to Chairman of the Board Don Gaston, is listed in the media guide on the same page.

After games, players usually go out to eat together, win or lose. Wives often meet at a restaurant or at someone's home, to socialize. They note the birthdays of each other's children and throw them parties. Occasionally the wives and kids even go along on road trips. Family participation isn't just tolerated by Celtics management, it's encouraged.

Every reporter who covers the Celtics, even briefly, comes away impressed by how little jealousy there is and by how close they continue to be.

"It carries over," says Togo Palazzi, a reserve forward on the Celtics' first championship team in 1957. "When you play for the Celtics, you feel like you're a part of it forever."

Former Celtics great Bob Cousy, now the team's TV broadcaster, watches a game with his wife.

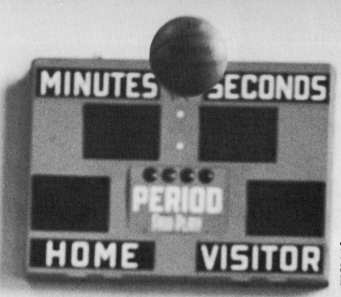

Former Celtics standout Sam Jones shoots some hoops during practice.

John Havlicek, Celtics star of the sixties and seventies, on the court during pregame warm-ups.

**The coaches oversee a
workout at rookie camp.**

Making the Team

The Celtics scouting team is headed by Jimmy Rodgers, the assistant coach, who, as this book was being put together, was named to succeed retiring head coach K. C. Jones. The chief scout is Forddy Anderson. Three of the assistant scouts are former Celtics players: Sam Jones, Rick Weitzman, and M. L. Carr.

Their written reports are augmented by information from various scouting organizations and by games taped from cable television. Red Auerbach also watches a lot of college games. Auerbach, as Celtics president, is ultimately responsible for what players make the team.

Says Rodgers: "We keep files on players who impress us as long as they're in school. This can start in a number of ways. A scout may see an underclass player while watching a senior. Or a college coach may tell us about a particular player. All the information is fed into our computer in the form of a rating system combining shooting, ball handling, speed, and attitude.

"Here's what we're looking for: (1) talent relevant to our system and needs; (2) team orientation; (3) intelligence, competitiveness, and durability; (4) the level of competition the player has faced. Most of all, though, we're looking for mental toughness. And you can't measure that until a player works against the pros."

The Celtics have always been known for favoring attitude over sheer physical ability.

In January, the scouting team holds a midseason conference to review its computer's findings. It decides at that time which players should be looked at more closely. The scouts then cover all the postseason tournaments, communicating with each oth-

Celtics management discusses the latest crop of college stars.

er two to three times a week. After the tournaments there is another meeting, at which a mock draft is held. This helps to narrow the possible choices further.

Celtics video coordinator Jon Jennings makes composite films of various players, including both their highlights and their low lights. The scouts want to study the players' weaknesses as well as their strengths. The final-selection meetings are held one week before the draft. A list is made then of the players the Celtics are really interested in.

Says General Manager Jan Volk: "There's no tie-breaking mechanism, no formal approach. We just talk and talk until we reach a consensus. By the time we've reached a decision, everybody's in agreement."

On June 22, 1987, Celtics management gathered at Boston Garden, where they were linked by phone to NBA draft headquarters in New York. They had been hoping a strong rebounding forward would be available for their first pick, the twenty-second in the draft. When none was, they took Reggie Lewis, a six-foot-seven-inch guard from Northeastern University. They believed Lewis could add height and speed to their aging backcourt. Then, on the second round, they took Brad Lohaus, a seven-foot center from Iowa, in hopes that Lohaus could replace Bill Walton, whose career had been plagued by injuries.

The Celtics made selections in each of the next five rounds. Occasionally an overlooked player, such as 1984 third-round pick Rick Carlisle, makes the team, but not often. In fact, the Celtics hold so little hope for the final rounds of the draft that they sometimes use them to make sentimental picks of Boston-area collegians or handicapped athletes.

After they had finished drafting, the Celtics immediately began contemplating roster changes based on the players they'd picked.

The Celtics don't like to trade players. It runs against their idea of family.

"You don't want players expecting trades all the time," says Volk. "It disrupts things. Plus it takes time

LF	19		KEN NORMAN
FRANK	20		JIM FARMER
TIZ	21		DALLAS COMEGYS
N WELP	22		REGGIE LEWIS
MURPHY	23		
CKSON			

**Representatives of all the NBA teams
gather for the college draft.**

for a new player to learn your system. If two teams trade players of equal value, both tend to get hurt for a while until the new players learn to fit in."

During the first week of August, the selection process for the team begins in earnest. That's when the draft choices and free agents report to the Celtics' annual rookie camp at Brandeis University. The free agents are former college players who have either spent the previous year in the Continental Basketball Association, played in Europe, been cut by another NBA team, or have done all three.

For ten days they scrimmage, hoping to impress the Celtics coaches. At rookie camp there are two practices daily, and after six practices the coaches have a pretty good sense of who won't make it. Last August three draft choices and two free agents were impressive enough to earn invitations to the regular preseason camp in early October.

Preseason camp is the spring training of basketball. It comprises three hard weeks of conditioning drills and exhibition games, during which stars struggle to get in shape and rookies fight to make the team.

In October, then-head coach K. C. Jones announced the twelve-man roster for the opening game of the season. For the 1987–88 season, two rookies, in addition to Reggie Lewis, had made the team: second-round pick Lohaus and Mark Acres, a six-foot-eleven-inch forward from Oral Roberts University who'd just played two seasons in Belgium. Acres was a 1985 second-round pick of the Dallas Mavericks who had been cut from their rookie camp.

Of the fourteen Celtics who had finished the 1986–87 season in June, only ten remained to begin the 1987–88 season in October. Nor would the cutting end there. By March of the new season, four more veterans would be gone, completing a 57 percent turnover of this most family-oriented team in less than nine months. And in May, in the midst of the play-offs, K. C. Jones himself would announce that he was retiring to take an executive position in the Celtics' front office.

Rookie: Brad Lohaus

I grew up in Arizona. When I was younger I hung out at the playground all day, sometimes right through dinner. I'd come home and fall asleep with my shoes and sweaty clothes on. We had a gravel driveway. That's why people say I never learned to dribble. I used to play one-on-one with my dad and with my brothers. I had my dad out there to play with and that probably kept me going at basketball.

The biggest difference playing here is the talent. In high school you maybe faced one good player on each team. You could always pick out the mismatches. Here there aren't many. It's basically talent against talent.

The thing I've had to get used to is the travel. We play Thursday night, travel, then play the next night. Mentally and physically you're worn out by the time you get to the next place. The veterans say you get used to it, but I don't know. Sometimes when you get out there you're not able to do what you did the night before. You have to adjust and change your game around. If your legs are gone and you're not able to jump, you have to do something else, maybe block your guy a little harder.

I was nervous before games at the beginning. Now it's not bad. You always wonder how you're going to play. But when you play you're out there reacting to what's going on. When you're shooting free throws you're just concerned with making them, not anything else. Not even the score. You just say, "I've got to make these two," and that's it. You just block everything else out. If you let it get to you, you're going to choke.

When I was coming to Boston, a lot of people said, "Hey, the veterans have their friends, and you're trying to knock them out of there. It's going to be rough." But it wasn't. The veterans were great; they accepted me as part of the team.

Brad Lohaus.

35

There's a lot of razzing that goes on, hazing. We rookies will get fined for something a veteran can do. Some veterans show up five minutes before practice. If I show up half an hour before practice everybody gets on me. Nothing goes by. You do something wrong and they'll catch you. If I get off a plane and I'm supposed to go left, and I go right, that's good for two weeks of razzing. It's constant, never-ending. The veterans are always looking for something to get the rookies on. I got fined for moving into Larry Bird's neighborhood without his permission. That was one hundred fifty dollars.

It's all just fun, of course. And all the veterans give me advice. Robert Parish works on the low post with me. Kevin McHale works on certain parts of my game. Larry Bird talks to me about game situations, like how to get open and get a shot off. And I get to play one-on-one with him. He'll call the shot before he shoots it. It's frustrating when he makes it. He's like a big brother to the rookies. He scolds us when we're bad, but then he has a good time with us.

Dennis Johnson has been giving me career advice, like how to deal with the press, and people bugging you in hotels and airports, and hecklers. One game, there was a guy behind the bench yelling at me. They usually get on the rookies on the road. I said something to him and DJ said: "Hey, forget about it." Then he turned around and yelled at him.

When I first came to town, I couldn't wait to play in Boston Garden. All the championship flags weren't up in the rafters because the circus was coming. So I got to see them all in the locker room, lying on the floor, right up close.

When we first played the Lakers I couldn't wait to get out there. I wanted to play against Jabbar because he was my hero. I'd written papers about him in high school. Then I played him. He scored on me twice, shot the patented hook shot on me. I figured I could tell my kids about that, the leading scorer in NBA history. He used that big hook shot on me. That's something. I'll remember that for a long time.

**Parish and Lohaus,
veteran and newcomer.**

Practice

The length and intensity of practices vary. Off-day practices include team scrimmages; game-day practices don't. Most practices are held at Hellenic College in Brookline, Massachusetts; some are held at Boston Garden.

A typical off-day practice begins at 11:30 A.M. At 9:45 Bill Walton is in the trainer's room, having his feet massaged. Players get treated and taped before practice, just as they do before a game. Larry Bird arrives at 10:00, wearing sweatpants and an emerald-green Celtics jacket. K. C. Jones and Fred Roberts come at 10:15, Dennis Johnson at 10:25. Roberts and Johnson soak their legs in the whirlpool, to warm the muscles. Bird hits the floor first, at 10:45, to shoot some baskets. By 11:20 the whole team is on the court, shooting.

Walton and Danny Ainge play one-on-one, challenging each other, laughing like kids. Bird stops

Bird begins practice by tossing an easy shot over his head.

K.C. Jones directs his
players.

shooting and looks on, grinning. K. C. Jones begins the practice with one short blast of his whistle, the signal for the trainer to begin leading the players in stretching exercises.

At 11:45 the assistant coaches set the defense for the next game, walking the players through their opponents' offense. One group of players acts the part of the opponents, another group guards them. The process looks like choreography. The players actually walk through the plays, as actors walk through their parts in rehearsal. K. C. Jones oversees them, stepping in whenever he sees something he doesn't like. He speaks quietly. The players pay close attention. He sometimes takes a player by the arm and moves him closer to where he wants him to be.

Then the Celtics practice some of their offense. They begin by running "weaves," or figure-eight patterns, down the floor, in groups of threes, ending in a lay-up. Then they do some set patterns—five men running, at a deliberate pace. The drills are partly to stretch their legs, partly to review the offense. Gradually it turns into a full-speed scrimmage, the starters against the subs.

According to Jimmy Rodgers, you can't tell from a practice how the veterans will do in a game. Scrimmaging is more important for bench players. Nonetheless, K. C. Jones decides which players to use, and for how long, by how they do in practice.

The scrimmage ends at 12:30. Some players go directly to the locker room, some continue shooting baskets, others play in pickup games. Sometimes, after a scrimmage, the losing team has to run "suicide drills," in which the players run back and forth, nearly the length of the court, several times. The winners stand on the sidelines teasing the losers—especially the slower centers and forwards—as they run.

Game-day practices are much shorter and are called "shoot-arounds," because that's how they end. In a shoot-around the team is divided into

Larry Bird and Red Auerbach, franchise player and franchise maker.

44

groups that compete against each other by shooting from various spots on the floor. The losers have to run a suicide drill.

Although all the scrimmages and drills are businesslike, before and after them the players act like kids on permanent recess. Such fooling around helps break the tension and monotony of the nine-month season and binds twelve different individuals into a team.

Danny Ainge likes to wear a shirt with the name "Lamar Mundain" on it. Lamar is a mythical playground character featured in advertising for an athletic footwear company. At one practice the team held an "other sports" day. Kevin McHale came dressed as a hockey player.

At the end of the season, when the team is tired, Larry Bird will sometimes bet the coach that he can make a shot from half court.

"For the day off," he says.

Danny Ainge wearing his "Lamar" shirt.

Equipment

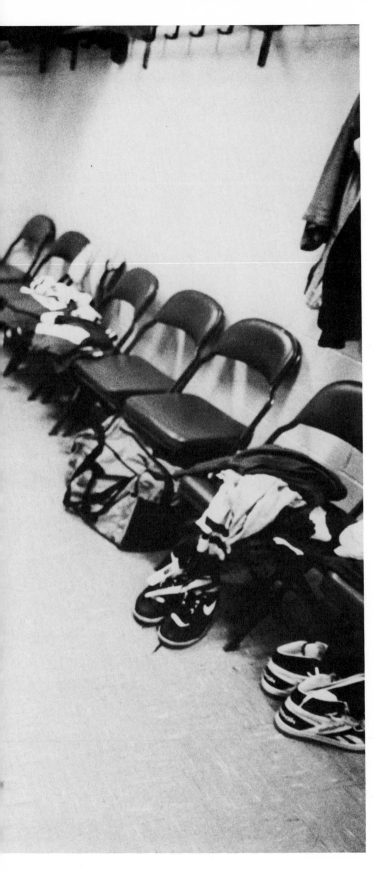

**Wayne Lebeaux laying
out uniforms on the road.**

Wayne Lebeaux is the Celtics equipment manager. He also doubles as road manager. Lebeaux got his start as a ball boy, then worked at the Boston Garden press gate for a year before becoming a locker-room assistant in 1984. When the Celtics' original equipment manager, Walter Randall, died in 1985, Lebeaux succeeded him. Frank Randall, Walter's son, now works for Lebeaux as an assistant.

On game days, Lebeaux often works from nine o'clock in the morning until midnight, taking care of players' needs. He runs the locker room, keeping it stocked with food and towels and soap, supplying uniforms and sneakers and basketballs. He's even been known to sleep in the locker room during a busy home stand. He spends most of each game in the locker room, watching the action on television.

Lebeaux supervises two assistants and seven ball boys. He hires ball boys from local high schools by calling up the principals. He asks for boys who are dependable, mature, and hard working. Ball boys stay for a season or two, sometimes longer. They provide water and towels for both the Celtics and their opponents during games. Two teams can often use more than five hundred towels during a game. Ball boys also get take-out food for the players when they're at home. On the road, or at practice,

Lebeaux delivers the food himself.

Basketball requires less equipment than any other major sport. The only recent innovation is the rebounding machine, which gathers and returns balls to the players during shooting drills. Otherwise, it's just the ball and the hoop.

The hoop is ten feet off the ground and eighteen inches in diameter. It has a white cord net that drops down fifteen to eighteen inches. The ball is thirty inches around and weighs twenty-one ounces. It is filled with air to a pressure of seven and a half to eight and a half pounds.

At the beginning of the season, each NBA team receives a shipment of official leather Spalding basketballs. Each ball has the team's identification stamped on it. New balls are broken in during practice. When new, the balls appear orange. With use, they become brown from the sweat on the players' hands. During the warm-up before each game, a referee chooses one of the practice balls and shows it to the captain of each team. (The Celtics captain is Larry Bird.) This ball is the only ball used during the game. The referee marks it with a pen and gives it to a member of the scoring crew at halftime, to keep the players from using it during second-half warm-ups. Usually, any given ball is used in a game four or five times during a season.

Each Celtics player has four uniforms, two white ones for home games and two green ones for road games. Each also goes through twenty-five or thirty pairs of sneakers a year. On the 1987–88 team, the Celtics player with the largest sneaker size was Artis Gilmore, size 18. Lebeaux orders sneakers from the various companies with which the players have contracts. For a number of years, the Celtics wore green sneakers. But because the sneakers were coming from different companies, the players were showing up wearing twelve different shades of green. So the Celtics went back to the black high-tops of their glory days, the fifties and sixties. If a company can't provide footwear in that color, Lebeaux will spray sneakers with black shoe paint.

The device under the hoop returns the ball to the shooter.

51

33 BIRD

Clean uniforms await the players before the game.

Training

If you or I were playing," says Dr. Robert Leach, prominent Boston orthopedic surgeon, "we'd be like cars traveling at five miles an hour. NBA players are like vehicles moving at one hundred miles an hour."

Keeping these vehicles moving, and fixing them when they crash, is the job of Celtics trainer Ed Lacerte.

Lacerte knew what he wanted to do from the time he was fourteen. He was a student trainer in high school, then took degrees in both athletic training and physical therapy at Boston University. After graduation, he was head trainer for BU's football and hockey teams, spent two years in private practice, and then became Celtics trainer in 1987.

Athletic training has changed a lot in recent years. It's no longer just a matter of tape and aspirin. Trainers are now members of sports medicine teams that include nutritionists, physical therapists, and strength coaches. And trainers now spend as much time preventing injuries as treating them, designing conditioning programs for players year-round.

All NBA trainers accompany their teams on the road. Some also act as traveling secretaries, making plane and hotel reservations for their teams. Lacerte arrives an hour and a half before each practice and three hours before each game. Before practice he leads the team in stretching exercises. Before both practices and games, he tapes ankles to prevent sprains and "mobilizes" feet, rolling the joints and stretching the tissues to make the muscles more pliable. Basketball players get sore feet and muscle strains from being up on their toes and running for forty minutes, and as many as six miles, during each game.

Lacerte also keeps a small box in the trainer's room for treating injuries with ultrasound and electrical stimulation. Ultrasound uses sound to introduce heat into a muscle. It's a long-term treatment. Electrical stimulation, a short-term treatment, relieves muscle spasms and swelling.

During the game Lacerte stays on the bench in case there's an injury or he needs to retape a player. When necessary, he pushes or pops dislocated fingers back into position. He also keeps track of free throws and time-outs, to help the coaches.

If there is a serious injury, the Celtics team physician, Dr. Arnold Scheller, is called in. Scheller sits beside the scorekeepers' table during home games and accompanies the team on the road during the play-offs.

After the game, Lacerte treats some players with a short version of their pregame routine. He also "ices" players and urges all to do more stretching, particularly if specific muscles are bothering them.

Lacerte never nags, though.

"Dealing with professional athletes is very different from handling high-school and college players. It's the maturity level. The Celtics have a knowledge of their bodies and what should be done. They're a lot more independent at this level. You don't tell them what to do. You try to discuss it with them and convince them. They're coming from a much wider experience. And they're adults."

The Celtics also have a consultant on eating, Nancy Clark, a registered dietitian and exercise physiologist. Clark develops diet programs for the players and meets with them occasionally to answer their questions.

Clark believes that, to ensure high performance, the ideal diet for a basketball player should be rich in carbohydrates and low in fat. Carbohydrates (potatoes, corn, rice, beans, bread, spaghetti) are excellent sources of energy, whereas fat, though it makes things taste good, doesn't help athletic performance at all.

Clark's recommended dietary formula for an athlete is 60 or 70 percent carbohydrates, 25 percent (or less) fat, and 15 percent protein.

Ballplayers won't give up all junk food, Clark realizes. So she suggests substitutions: pretzels instead of potato chips, fig bars instead of chocolate chips, and cheaper brands of ice cream, which are lower in fat.

To Clark, what players eat before a game isn't as important as what they eat for breakfast and after a game.

"What you eat the morning of a game will be digested. Hopefully, it will be a food that's high in carbohydrates, like cereal, muffins, pancakes, or French toast. It'll get stored in the form of glycogen, which is muscle sugar, and be ready to go when you are.

"The postgame meal is also important. In the first two to four hours after hard exercise, the muscles are most able to replace the glycogen. Again, you need carbohydrates so that your muscles can recover for the next day. Very lean red meat can also be helpful. It's an excellent source of iron, which prevents anemia, and zinc, which helps heal injuries.

"Basketball players also should watch out for dehydration. They need lots of water and juices. They're big—they get really hot and they sweat heavily during games. Afterward, they have to be sure to replace the fluids, and always with water or juice first."

But Clark is no big fan of vitamins and food supplements.

"Supplements are more for the mind. If you believe in them, they might work for you. But no supplement can compensate for poor eating. I tell the players that any sort of deficiency can be corrected by adding or replacing certain foods. Trust the food, knowing that food works."

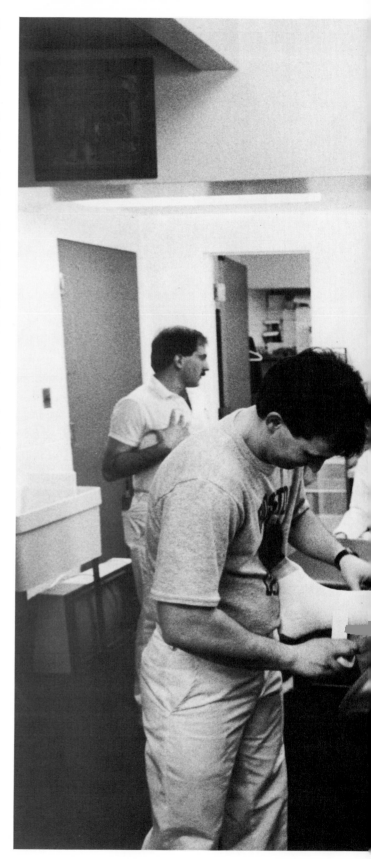

Trainer Ed Lacerte tapes up Robert Parish before a game.

Conditioning

Basketball players don't have to exercise during the season. Playing eighty-two games keeps them in shape.

Once the season ends, though, they are advised to take a few weeks off before beginning to alternate various forms of exercise, such as swimming and bicycling, rather than playing more basketball.

Robert Parish practices martial arts, which improves his balance. Kevin McHale swam after he had an operation on his foot and did resistance exercises in the water to strengthen particular muscles. Danny Ainge, a natural athlete, swims forty brisk laps a day to keep his wind up. He also rides a bike ten or fifteen miles several times a week.

To stay in shape, some NBA players take part in summer leagues. They must get the permission of their teams to play in these leagues and take out insurance to cover themselves in case of injury.

Danny Ainge works at staying fit.

In October, Celtics players are expected to arrive at preseason camp in shape, flexible, and with good endurance, ready to play.

During the first six days in camp there are two practices daily, one to one and a half hours each. One good conditioning drill is the continuous fast break, three men on two. The first time down the floor the players pass the ball rather than dribble; the next time they dribble. To keep the bench players sharp, assistant coach Chris Ford often organizes three-man games after practice. In one variation, the offense can't cross half court with the ball until all its players have crossed it. This forces each player to run faster in order to make the offense work.

Many players who've been traded to the Celtics are amazed at the intensity of their workouts. Some, like Willie Naulls, have passed out during the first day of drills. According to *Sports Illustrated's* Frank Deford, "historically, the Celtics have had a tremendous advantage because Red Auerbach whipped them into such shape. They had much more demanding early practices. As a result, they'd have great early-season records."

For the 1987–88 season, the most famous Celtics player of all, Larry Bird, made over his entire body.

Bird's off-season program was developed by Dan Dyrek, a physical therapist and consultant to the Celtics. Dyrek began treating Bird three years ago when Larry injured his back. Besides a bad back, Bird had tendonitis in both legs as well as an old elbow injury that would become aggravated whenever he threw floor-length passes. When Dyrek began treating him, Bird hadn't done a conditioning program in years.

Dyrek developed one for him. Its aims were: (1) Flexibility. Bird wasn't limber enough and so was prone to injury. (2) Body strength. This was necessary to help Bird battle under the boards and withstand the wear and tear of the long season. (3) Nutrition. Larry was eating too much junk food and red meat and was fifteen to twenty pounds overweight. (4) Endurance.

Vigorous sprinting is part of every practice.

Bird worked out three hours a day, five days a week.

He would begin with at least ten to fifteen minutes of stretching, some days for as long as an hour. He worked with free weights, ran, pedaled a stationary bike, and jumped rope. To avoid overworking particular muscles, he lifted weights on alternating days, working thirty to ninety minutes at a stretch. He used relatively low weight with many repetitions rather than fewer repetitions and high weight, which builds bulk as well as strength.

One routine called for Bird to pedal a stationary bike while lifting dumbbells, get off the bike and lift more weights, and then skip rope. Some days he would spend an hour or longer doing speed work on a track, running 440s, 220s, and 100-yard sprints. He also did road running, including jaunts along a course that rose gradually to one mile in elevation.

"When Larry saw the positive changes," says Dyrek, "he decided to do everything right and get the benefit from a nutritional program. He started eating a better, more balanced diet, cut down on red meat, added more fish and pasta, and began eating huge salads. By August, he was in incredible shape. He could do splits like a cheerleader, he'd lost fifteen pounds, his muscle tone was pronounced, and he felt terrific."

Stretching is an important way to avoid injuries.

Technician

Jon Jennings is the Celtics video coordinator. He graduated from Indiana University, where he worked for coach Bobby Knight. While in school he did video work for the Indiana Pacers. He began working full-time for the Celtics during the 1987–88 season.

Jennings tapes opponents' games from TV. He diagrams their offense so that the coaches can figure out what will work successfully against each team. The coaches themselves are constantly watching tapes, but Jennings is another eye.

During games, Jennings keeps detailed statistics on what is working for the Celtics. He sits directly behind the coaches, charting the offense by type of shot and by the player who attempted it. At halftime Jennings gives the results to the coaches, usually confirming what they already sense in their guts.

The Celtics have about thirty offensive plays with as many as five options on each. Plays are introduced gradually throughout the season. The Celtics tend to run plays in clusters, using only a few every night so that they can show the next opponent a new look.

During a recent game against Washington, Jennings leaned over to tell Jimmy Rodgers that the "42" play was working well. Forty-two is a double screen for Larry Bird. Rodgers told then head-coach K. C. Jones, who immediately jumped up and signaled "42" (four fingers, two fingers) to Dennis Johnson, who was pushing the ball down the floor.

Jon Jennings sits behind the bench and charts the offense.

DJ slowed down and signaled "42." Bird didn't see the signal, so both assistant coaches shouted "42." Bird got the pass, shot, and scored. Jennings wrote "33" (Bird's number) with a circle around it next to "42" on his sheet.

About 50 to 75 percent of the offense during a game develops from set patterns. The rest is improvised. Opponents know much of the Celtics' offense. They recognize a "42" when they see it developing or when it is signaled. But everything happens so quickly that they usually don't have time to react.

When the Celtics are defending the basket near their bench, the coaches shout out the names of opponents' plays as they see them developing. The coaches' voices are so familiar they cut right through the crowd noise to the players.

The day after a game, Jennings summarizes the Celtics' offense and feeds this information into a computer. He keeps a file on each of the opponents, noting how the Celtics did against them in a particular game and in the previous three times they met. The coaches get these offensive summaries the next time they play those opponents, to remind them of what works best against that team.

Jennings did not play basketball in college. He was, however, on his junior-high-school chess team, and he likes to think of basketball as a high-speed version of chess.

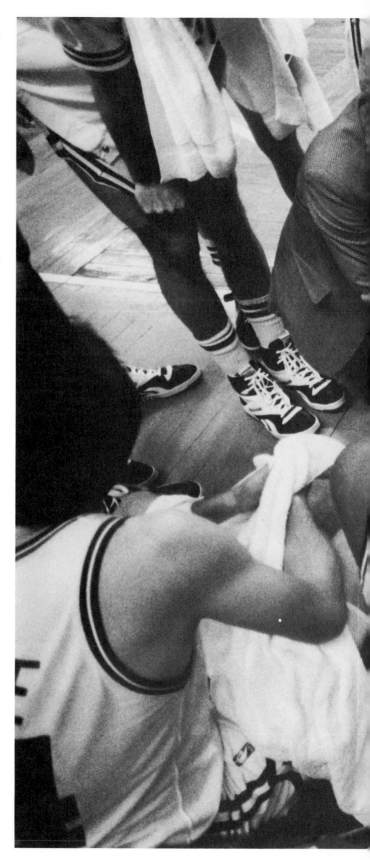

The coaches often use Jennings's insights in plotting game strategy.

Strategy

The offense of recent Celtics teams has been designed around six basic strengths: Larry Bird's versatility, Kevin McHale's post-up offense, Robert Parish's inside finesse, Danny Ainge's range, Dennis Johnson's point guard power, and the speed of the bench.

The Celtics like to isolate Bird one-on-one. He shoots like a guard, goes to the basket like a forward, and always finds the open man when he's double-teamed.

Diagram 1 illustrates the Celtics' classic "pick-and-roll" play. Parish screens Bird's defender. Bird either shoots off the screen, passes back to Parish if he's double-teamed, or drives to the basket if the defenders get confused.

Diagram 2 shows the "two and three man play." Dennis Johnson has the ball. On a count, Ainge and Bird peel off, setting up a pass to the post. Sometimes they fake this move and cut backdoor to the basket.

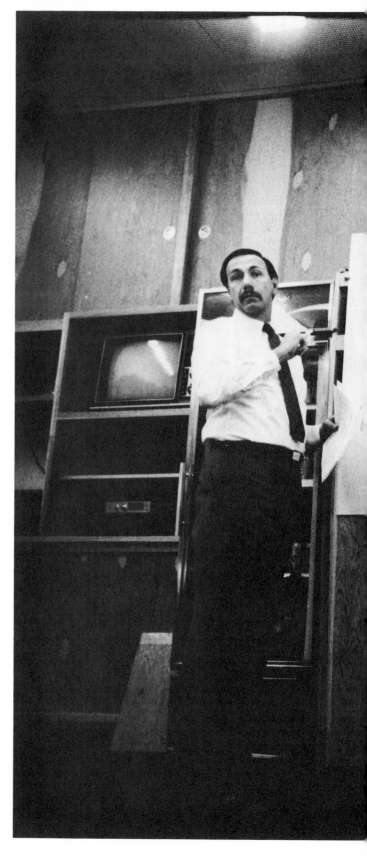

Assistant coach Chris Ford diagrams the opponents' offense.

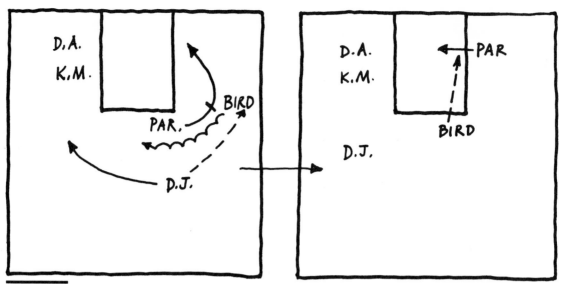

Diagram 1: pick-and-roll.

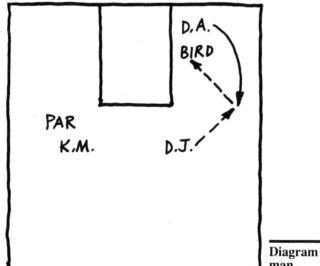

Diagram 2: two and three man.

PASS — — — →
DRIBBLE ∿∿∿→
CUT ——————→

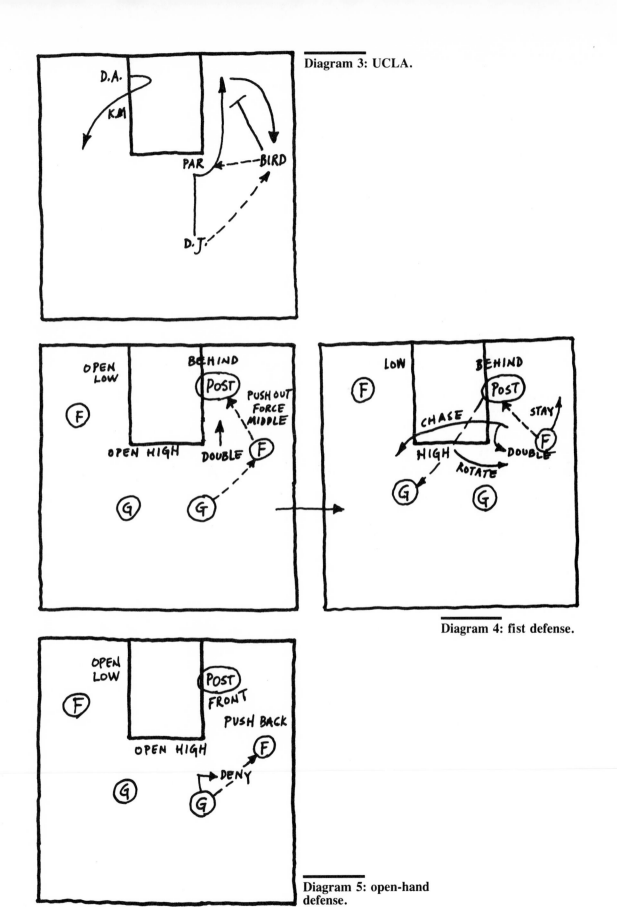

Diagram 3: UCLA.

Diagram 4: fist defense.

Diagram 5: open-hand defense.

Diagram 3 illustrates the "UCLA" play. Johnson passes to Bird and cuts to the basket. Bird can shoot, hit Johnson posting up, pass to Ainge fanning out on the wing or to Parish for a pick and roll or backdoor lob.

All of this changes when the subs come in.

"We want the bench to play conservatively," says K. C. Jones. "They aren't out there to be superstars; we're just looking for mistake-free minutes."

On defense, the Celtics mix individual skills with a strong team concept.

"We'll overplay the man with the ball and all players on the strong side in some schemes," says Jones. "In other approaches, we'll double down aggressively, making it difficult for an important low-post scorer. We also try to run a great scorer like Michael Jordan into as many traps as possible."

The Celtics use two basic defenses.

Diagram 4 illustrates the "fist" defense, which has Celtics defenders overplaying their man and all opponents on the side of the court where the ball is. This is an aggressive defense which is designed to set the tempo and control the passing lanes.

Diagram 5 illustrates the "open-hand" defense. This is a "help-out" approach. It tries to force an outside shot by having the defenders sink back toward the basket, making passes to the inside difficult.

When the opposing team is not working a set play but is moving on the break, each Celtics player covers one area and stays with his man in that area for the entire play. In the half-court game the Celtics are encouraged to switch in the "fist" defense, but stay with their man in the "open hand."

Coaches Rodgers and Jones swap observations during practice.

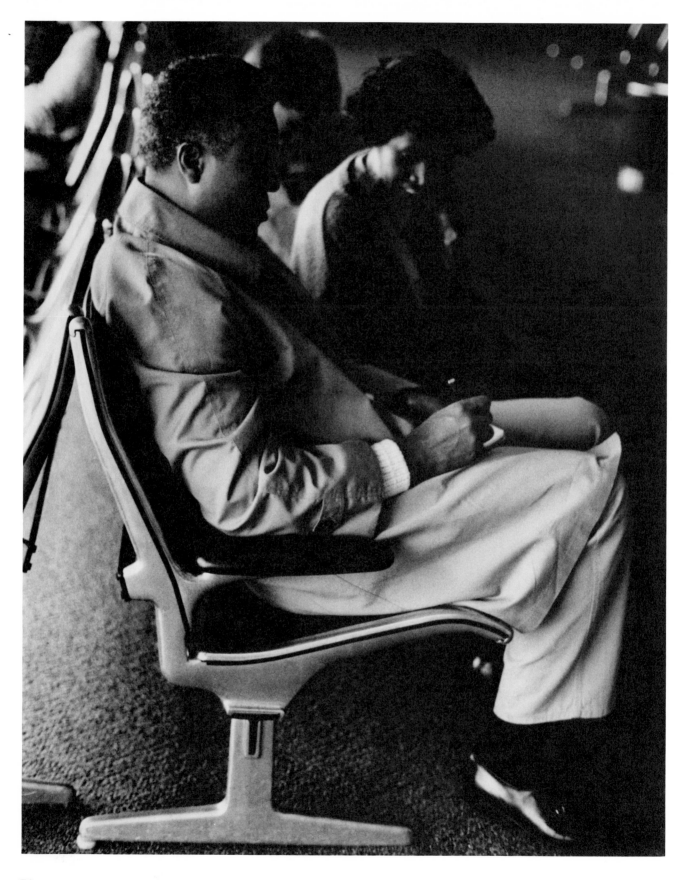

Coach: K. C. Jones

Cutting players is the worst part, particularly with these players, who have gone through what they have to get here, playgrounds to junior high, high school, college, then to the pros, accomplishing all that. And then to be told, "You're not good enough to make it." It's always hard to tell people they're not good enough. I've been through the same thing, or close to it. So I know the feeling. And being traded is almost like being cut, if a player's been someplace a long time. It's like a slap in the face.

Everyone I cut I see personally. I never call them on the phone. That's hiding. You have to face up to the bad side. The rookies are stunned, they just kind of sit there. Of course, it's started to build up in that player as it gets closer to cut time. There are little indications that tell him things are not going well. And then he's called in. And so he's disappointed, stunned, that kind of thing. Although some expect it.

No one ever tries to talk me out of it. It's an inevitable thing. You just tell them, "I'm going to release you." It's never easy. Afterward you can tell them, "Try this, try that, you have the tools." Then, that's the extent of it, boom, that's it. What I try to do is give them some avenues they can follow, the Continental Basketball Association, what that could do for you, Europe or other teams. But the longer you keep them in the office, the worse the situation gets. You can talk before cutting someone and have a conversation after you cut them, and it really doesn't do any good.

I was almost cut from the Celtics myself, as a rookie. It came down to two people, myself and Gene Conley, who was 6 feet 9 inches, a backup to Bill Russell, and we didn't have another backup center at the time. I knew I was going to be cut because why would they keep me, a guy who can't

K. C. Jones signs autographs at the airport.

75

shoot and who's too short? You had a six-foot-nine-inch guy here who could bang around and get rebounds. All I could feel was fear. It was real simple. Fear of being cut. And if I am cut, what do I do, where do I go?

My coaching style is low-key. Somehow it's expected that you need to yell to coach. It goes on in the business world too. But if you yell at someone and call them ignorant or dumb, you're going to lose. What that does is take away confidence and creativity.

Red Auerbach would yell and scream. But he never called anyone dumb, or berated someone in front of the team. What he had was the ability to cause fear, which is a great tool to have. Red knew how to use that to wake you up, not to hurt anyone. Laid-back can accomplish the same thing, if you go right to the problem.

When I do get loud at times, it's not personal. I'm speaking to the individuals involved through the whole group rather than singling out someone. I talk about what we're doing and who we are. That's the extent of my yelling.

It's important that the players understand what the coaches are saying, but it's more important that they understand each other. That's the beginning of teamwork right there, that they work for each other. You get it across in different ways. A player shouldn't criticize his teammate. That's destructive. Any criticism should come from the coach. Since I've been with the Celtics, as a player and a coach, I've never heard one player criticize his teammate. Totally the opposite. If a player throws a bad pass, his teammate will say, "Don't worry about it." If he's shooting and missing, they'll say, "You're a great shooter, take some more shots." That kind of support. What that gives a teammate is confidence. The minute you criticize a teammate for a bad pass, "You missed me," or "What did you take that shot for," now you've got two guys in the game who are angry at each other. You've got three guys playing against five.

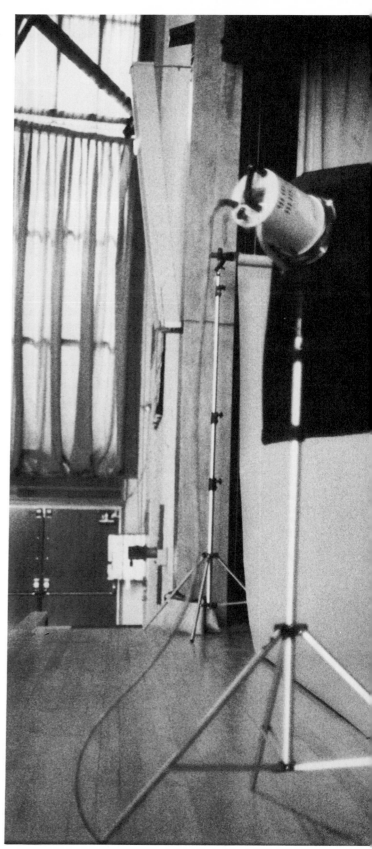

Coach Jones poses for a public-service announcement with some young friends.

Championship flags
hang from the rafters
at Boston Garden.

Home

The Celtics, with their emphasis on team play and their family-oriented work ethic, are a throwback to an earlier era. So is their home.

Boston Garden was built in 1928 by sports promoter Tex Rickard, who planned to construct six imitation Madison Square Gardens around the country. Boston Garden is the only one he ever completed.

For sixty years the Garden has housed basketball at every level. For thirty of those years it has been considered obsolete—too small, without air conditioning, with not enough good seats, and in too unsavory a location. Still, it has character. So every year its owners slap a fresh coat of paint on it, every year the latest "new arena" plan is shelved, and every year the Celtics come home to Boston Garden.

The Celtics offices are next door at 150 Causeway Street, on the eighth floor. There are ten small rooms and an informal, homey atmosphere. Behind the receptionist's desk is a picture of Red Auerbach, smiling, with cigar. The offices have blond-wood doors and emerald-green rugs.

On the reception-area walls are Celtics team pictures, from 1946–47 to the present. Sixteen pictures have championship ribbons. In the earliest picture, the Celtics wear short-sleeved jerseys and striped stockings like a nineteenth-century baseball team.

Auerbach's office, which is the largest, is crammed with photographs and mementos, including a Washington Capitols jacket from his first coaching job and a life-size cutout of Red himself. The view from his window is of Boston's grimy Southeast Expressway. The office is separated from a conference room by a sliding glass door. Red and team owner Don Gaston often eat in this conference room before night games—cold cuts, chicken wings, and Swedish meatballs—before descending by elevator to the game.

The Celtics locker room is just a few steps from the basketball court. There is no sign on its door. Outside it stands Grant Gray, a Boston special police officer who has worked at the Garden for twenty-five years. He allows the press to come in before and after games. Sometimes people try to talk their way in.

" 'I've got a message for Larry Bird,' they'll say, or 'I'm Larry's cousin.' Larry seems to have a lot of cousins."

The locker room itself is a surprisingly small space, about fourteen paces lengthwise, with dressing areas for all the players along three walls. Each player's name and number is printed on a small green plaque that hangs above his area. Veterans and rookies are mixed together. There is a chair in front of each locker. The rug is the same emerald shade as the one in the offices.

On the wall opposite the lockers are two TVs for watching tapes and near the water cooler is a triangular piece of wood, angled, on which the players stretch their calves. In the room's center is a table. After the game, the players take turns coming out of the trainer's room to sit on this table and talk to the press.

Some consider Boston Garden small and obsolete, but it has plenty of character.

Nearby is the trainer's room, which has padded tables, a whirlpool, and an ice machine for ice packs. Next door is the coaches' room, inside which is the masseur's table. There's also a separate shower room with several toilets. The ball boys stock this room with razors and shaving cream in case the players forget to bring their own.

The visitors' locker room is down the corridor from that of the Celtics. The contrast is hilarious. It's painted battleship gray. The floor is linoleum. There are wooden pegs to hang clothes on and an open, wooden shelf area above. The visitors sit on plain benches along the walls. Half of the room has a high ceiling, the other half is low. It's like being in a cave. Visitors' locker rooms are similar all over the league. It's part of what is meant by "home-court advantage."

The Floor

It's the most famous floor in professional sports.

There is always ice beneath the Celtics' parquet floor during the regular season, for hockey games. The ice is kept frozen by pipes filled with glycol, the same fluid used in refrigerators. Whenever the Celtics aren't playing, the parquet must be taken up, for hockey or boxing, ice shows or rock concerts. The changeovers occur almost daily.

Dennis Grabowski, general foreman of the Boston Garden, is in charge. The work is done by a twenty-five-member crew of men and women called the "bullgang." There are four full-time Garden employees on the bullgang and twenty-one part-timers, or "casuals." The casuals must report to work two hours after a Celtics tip-off. But many come to see the whole game and are given free standing-room admission.

Within ten minutes after the game ends, as the crowd is still leaving, two workmen with drills begin removing the recessed screws in the parquet floor. They are trailed by another worker who tosses the screws into buckets. The floor has 264 pieces. Each five-by-five-foot piece weighs 150 pounds and is held in place by four screws.

"Removing them is a back-breaking job," says Grabowski. "You're bent over the whole time. Kenny Davis, who's seventy-two and has been here for thirty-two years, can go much faster than a young guy who's not used to it. Kenny's brother-in-law, Stanley Kolpaczynski, is our oldest worker. He's seventy-eight."

Teams of four workers lift the individual pieces and stack them on one of twenty-one carts. Two tractors roar in and out of the Garden, pulling the

The "bull gang" starts dismantling the floor right after the game.

carts behind them. The pieces are marked on the edges so that they can be quickly put down again in place. The parquet floor rests on a subfloor, which protects it from the ice. Pieces of this floor are also carted away to the storage hall next to the arena.

Meanwhile, other crew members take up the twenty-five hundred extra chairs that surround the floor during Celtics games. It takes about an hour to pick up the basketball floor and two hours to turn the arena into a hockey rink. It takes an hour and a half to replace the floor (because the pieces must be lined up and fastened) and two and a half hours to turn the rink back into a basketball court.

The last things to be put in place are the baskets and backboards. They are attached to a pneumatically operated frame. When a key is turned, this frame either moves up or folds down.

Every year during the play-offs the crew repaints the parquet floor, buffs it with steel wool, and finishes it with polyurethane. Last year, Bobby Davis of Charlestown repainted the leprechaun logo at center court.

The wood used in the floor was bought after World War II from the Lynn shipyard by the Celtics' first owner, Walter Brown. Because it is so old it has many dead spots, which increase after the hockey season ends. The ice is melted and drained at that

To complete this job in under two hours takes great teamwork. The backboard comes down, the screws are removed, and the floor comes up in sections.

time, and the parquet floor is put on cement, which is even more uneven.

"There's all little peaks and valleys in it," says Grabowski, "so we have to spruce up a spot, make it half an inch higher or lower. We put wooden cleats underneath to even things out."

During games there is considerable wear and tear on the floor. During every changeover, three to five pieces have to be repaired. The Garden employs a carpenter to work full-time on the floor.

"You got these big guys who weigh 250 pounds jumping around on it," says Grabowski. "Some-

The floor before . . . times an insert lets go. When this happens, a piece

of the floor becomes looser. The spot goes dead—
you can actually feel it give, it rattles around."

Most of the casuals begin by knowing someone
who is already doing changeovers. Dennis Grabowski's father was a casual. Casuals are currently
paid $8.77 an hour.

"But they get paid for three and a half hours,
regardless. So they work on incentive. The faster
they work, the faster they're out of here. Our record
for a complete changeover is one hour and twenty
minutes. But sometimes it takes longer. They came
in last night at eleven and left at three in the
morning—all for about thirty dollars."

. . . and after.

Television

The truck arrives first. It must be powered up by 12:30 P.M. for a 7:30 game. The truck driver—who lives the life of a nomad, driving to events as far west as Michigan—secures a spot outside Boston Garden, crawls into a small area in the cab, and sleeps.

An engineer sometimes travels with him. Otherwise, the engineer flies to the event and meets the truck. Boston Garden is considered hostile territory for a TV truck. It's difficult to find a parking space on Causeway Street, and more equipment is stolen there than outside any other arena on the East Coast.

The truck needs power to run its equipment. So the engineer runs a line to a second-floor closet in Boston Garden and plugs it in. An hour later, the camera crew arrives. The crew includes Richard Garrett, a free-lance cameraman who operates one of the five cameras for a typical game.

The crew moves the cameras and other equipment into the Garden on carts. There are 7500 feet of cable for the cameras alone. Sometimes Garrett helps the audio engineers tape a microphone under the basket. This microphone picks up the sound of the ball hitting the rim or making a *swish* sound as it passes through the net. To pick up court noise, another microphone is held by a "grip" who sits on the floor near center court.

Garrett operates the camera by holding it on his shoulder under the basket. This camera also has a microphone, which picks up the sounds of the players shouting to each other, their sneakers squeaking, and the crowd cheering.

All the equipment is ready three or four hours before the game. The truck crew runs a test, then heads to a restaurant to eat. The producer and director arrive about two hours before game time. The producer arranges a player interview, which

Cameraman Richard Garrett often finds himself in the thick of the action.

Garrett shoots at center court about ninety minutes before tap-off.

During the game, Garrett must follow all the action, looking especially for spectacular plays that can be replayed. He also covers the coaches close up on the bench. Sometimes the action spills over to where Garrett sits. Three or four times in recent years players have crashed into him, knocking him and his camera head over heels.

People often tell Garrett he's lucky to be able to watch games close up. "I really like doing this," he says. "But when you're working, you don't get to watch the game. You're too busy looking for the best possible shot. There are times I have no idea what the score is. The Celtics could be ahead by twenty points and I don't know it."

The director sits in the truck's tiny control room, watching a bank of small TV screens numbered one to five. These numbers correspond to the cameras, two above the court, one at center court, and one behind each basket. The director changes the camera angles by calling the number to the "switcher" who sits next to him.

The producer sits beside the director, talking to the announcers through their headsets and to the three tape-replay operators sitting in another room inside the truck. In the same room a video engineer sits at a panel, making sure that colors are adjusted and that the picture is in focus and well lighted.

In the control room, behind the director, is a technician, who uses a special machine to type up the information that appears on the bottom of the TV screen. Behind him is the audio engineer, who controls the volume on the different microphones on the court. He also plays the telecast's theme music by punching a button, over his head, that operates a cartridge.

After the game, it takes the crew about an hour to break down the equipment and pack it into the truck. Often, as they are doing this, the Boston Garden crew is taking apart the parquet floor. So it looks as if the entire Garden is being packed up and carted away.

**The camera above the court
captures the flow of the game.**

Road Trip

The Celtics, like all NBA teams, play forty-one regular-season games on the road. Except for two West Coast swings, however (one consisting of seven games in ten nights, the other of five games in nine nights), their trips include just one or two games.

Wayne Lebeaux, the equipment manager, picks up airplane tickets and hotel reservations from the team's travel agent. He then drives to the airport in a van loaded with ten to fourteen large canvas bags full of uniforms and equipment. He's at the departure gate one and a half hours before flight time collecting boarding passes, which he hands to the players as they arrive.

The players drive themselves to the airport. According to league rules, they must travel first class.

Professional basketball teams travel with surprisingly little equipment.

Sometimes first class is full and players get bumped. Rookies get bumped first. When this happens, Lebeaux makes sure they get aisle seats for their long legs. Because most road trips are short, the players are able to take along their personal effects in carry-on luggage.

On the road the players read, play cards, or listen to music on portable CD players. Bird, Johnson, Ainge, and Gilmore often play a card game called "tonk." McHale and Ed Lacerte, the trainer, play cribbage.

When the plane lands the players are met by a bus, which has been chartered for the whole trip. The bus takes them to their hotel. At the hotel Lebeaux collects the room keys and hands them to the players.

Each player has his own room during the season. During the preseason, players double up and are assigned randomly to rooms by Lebeaux. Lebeaux also takes care of the press and radio accommodations. On a typical trip he has twenty-eight people in his care. The players stay on one floor of the hotel, the staff on another, and the media on another. The

On the plane, *Boston Globe* sportswriter Bob Ryan talks with Celtics general manager Jan Volk.

players fraternize with the press to some extent. But whereas the radio announcers are considered part of the family, the press isn't.

The players nap or eat meals in their rooms. At 6:00 P.M. they go downstairs to board the bus for the arena. If tap-off is at 8:30, they begin their physical preparations in the visitors' locker room at 6:30, taping, stretching, and so forth. They also watch tapes of their opponents on a VCR.

At 6:45 the coaches begin diagraming plays on a blackboard. At 7:00 they hold a team meeting, a low-key discussion of strategy. Just before 8:00 the players hit the floor to begin their pregame warm-ups. After the game they shower quickly, dress, and talk to the press. Then it's onto the bus and back to the hotel or directly to the airport and the next city.

On off days, movies are a favorite pastime. Players either go out to a theater together or stay in their rooms watching TV movies. Rookies are more likely to wander around new cities, shopping or seeing the sights. Because they're not famous, they're less likely to be pestered by fans. Larry Bird rarely travels more than a block from his hotel for dinner because fans hound him so much.

Each player gets thirty-nine dollars a day in meal money. There is a loosely enforced dress code: "neat" clothing, including shoes; no sneakers, no T-shirts. Although the veterans tend to like road trips the least, Bill Walton says he likes everything about basketball: "the road trips, the practices, the routine, all of it, just getting up and doing it every day."

Before the game, players suit up in the visitors' locker room at Madison Square Garden.

After the game, Larry Bird soaks his feet in ice water and takes questions from the media.

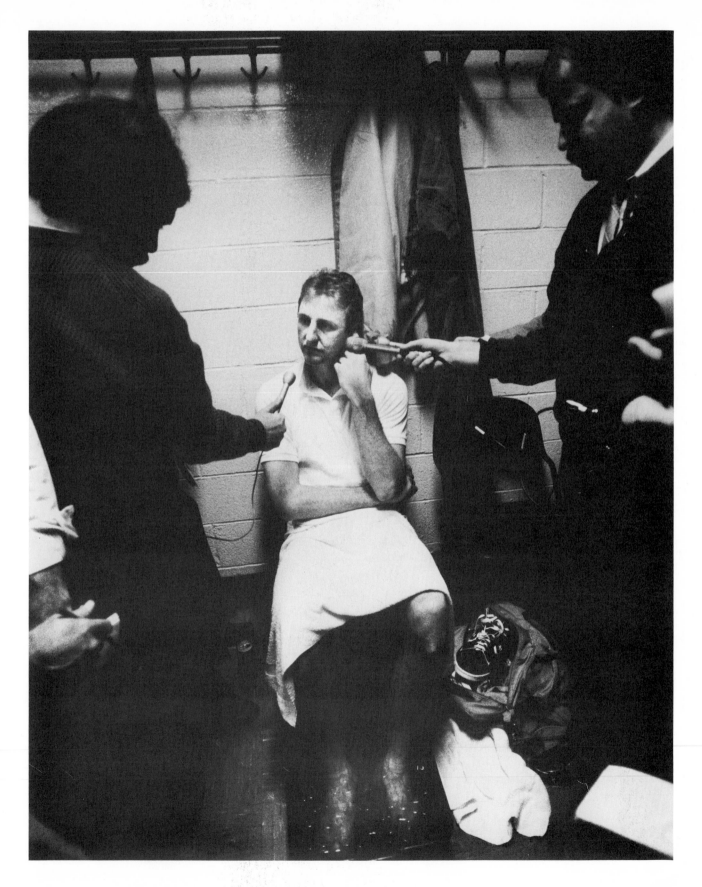

Fines,
Jokes,
Tickets,
Opponents

Assistant coach Chris Ford levies fines. Players are fined five dollars for each foul shot missed. Despite their high salaries, players "still don't like paying it," says Ford, "so it helps them concentrate a little harder on free throws." Players are also fined five dollars a minute if they are late for practice or for the team bus. Ford collects the fines on road trips. "As soon as they get their meal money from the equipment manager, I play Grim Reaper. That way they can't say they don't have any cash." The fines go toward a Celtics picnic at the end of the year.

Practical jokes are usually played on rookies. In the preseason, rookies have their names attached to their warm-up jackets with Velcro instead of being sewn on. Veterans turn the names upside down, and the rookies run out on the court wearing them that way. When the players line up before a

Moses Malone applies a bear hug to Kevin McHale.

98

Detroit's Bill Laimbeer
grins, but arch-rival
Robert Parish is all
business on the court.

game, the veterans send the rookies out first, then leave them standing there alone to be gawked at by the crowd. Veterans tell rookies the wrong time to meet the bus so that the rookies arrive early. Veterans convince rookies that it's part of their job to carry everybody's luggage on road trips, and the rookies obey until they catch on.

Each Celtics player gets two free tickets to every home game. If he needs extra tickets for a particular game, he can swap or borrow another player's. Former Celtics players do not have to pay to attend games.

Who are the Celtics' toughest individual opponents?

Larry Bird finds Michael Cooper a fierce defend-

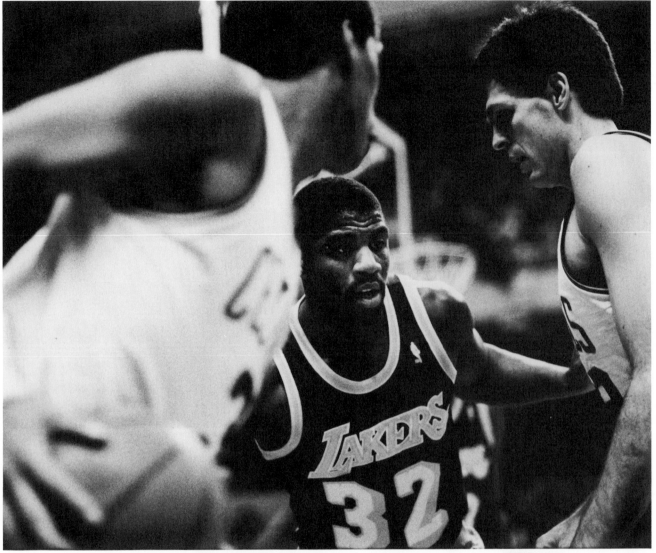

Magic Johnson is always tough on Celtics guards.

er. "He's tough mentally and tries to deny me the ball." On defense, Larry considers Bernard King and Dominique Wilkins the least appealing assignments.

Wilkins is also Kevin McHale's biggest challenge. He least likes being guarded by the Dallas duo of Sam Perkins and James Donaldson.

Danny Ainge rates opposing guards like this: Michael Jordan, Magic Johnson, Isiah Thomas.

Dennis Johnson also puts Jordan at the top, followed closely by Magic Johnson and Sidney Moncrief.

Moses Malone is the center who forces Robert Parish to play hardest. But he believes Akeem Olajuwon is "the most challenging young player in the league."

Some other tough foes: Patrick Ewing, Dominique Wilkins, Byron Scott.

Larry Bird manages to get a shot off.

Veteran:
Dennis Johnson

I began playing at Emerson Elementary School in Compton, California. But I used to roam all over the area playing, anywhere I could find a game. I liked basketball because it was so fast-moving and exciting. It was a way of expressing myself when I was a kid. I could let all my emotions show in whatever I did out there, dribbling, shooting, rebounding, playing defense.

Growing up, I had starry eyes like most kids. I used to say to myself, "I want to be like those guys on television." Little did I know it's much more of a grind than you think when you're young.

Now, I'm still the bright-eyed man who came into the league. I still have ambitions—if you lose your dream you lose everything—and the game is absolutely still fun. But I see it more in perspective. After four or five years, it becomes a job. You have lots of good times, but there are bad times too.

Like the hecklers on the road. It's the same hecklers over the years. Always, always. Sooner or later you get tired of it. Your mind just blows up on you every now and then. You can always hear these people. Then you have teams you don't play well against. And you can have personality clashes with your teammates, if you're on a team playing under .500. Don't ever wind up on a team below .500. You get players who'll do anything to get out of that place.

As far as the fans are concerned, basketball is a sport, but it's also entertainment. For some people, it's what they look forward to, the culmination of their work day. People live and die to go to the game

**Dennis Johnson knows
that dealing with the
press is part of his job.**

after work. I go outside and there are the same people who have gotten my autograph night in and night out for the last five or six years and that's hard for me to understand.

I've had people come up and tell me, "I think you're so wonderful, we live and die for you." And my answer is, "I'm just like you. I may play basketball, but I'm a man just like you." They say, "Yeah, yeah, I know that, but I still really admire you guys." I say, "Thank you very much." There's no answer you can give them because they already have a fix in their head about what and who you are.

It's hard to understand all the adulation, but it's nice to be accepted and it makes you feel good. After your career is over, that's the hard part. Every player has to deal with that. It's different with every player how they're going to handle that.

As for trades, nobody likes it, but it's a business. If it happens, it happens. I'd still stay friends with people on this team. You don't have many years in the league. You can't worry about that. You just play, every day, as hard as you can. It's like any job: you shouldn't do it with half an effort because you're worrying about what the boss will think, because if you do, then that's when the boss will start to notice.

No one explicitly says to a rookie, "You've got to be a team player." But when they see that Larry has a ten-footer, and he passes it to me for a two-footer, that tells them right there. You say it by example. Then they do the same thing, and if not, we give them a pat on the back and say, "Hey look, the other guy was open two feet away from you. . . ."

I love the competition. I get up for every game. Off the court my demeanor is different. You get along with your opponents there; you're friends. When I shoot a free throw in a pressure situation it's only me and the rim. The only thing that could possibly bother me is a gun going off in the arena. If I miss, my teammates know I've tried my best; nothing's ever held against you. I love it. There's nothing like being tied with two minutes to go in a game. I just have this feeling in my body of time shrinking.

One thing a veteran knows is when and how much to argue.

Autograph hunters swarm around Johnson after practice.

Game Day

On a typical game day, Larry Bird arrives first, by 5:00 P.M. for a 7:30 game. He goes to the trainer's room, where the trainer works on his lower back, feet, ankles, and elbow. Bird then does some stretching exercises. At 5:30 he and assistant equipment manager Joe Qatato walk the few steps to the court. Qatato, twelve inches shorter than Bird, brings a rack of balls. His job is to catch the ball as it swishes through the basket, or retrieve it if it misses, and fire it back to Bird. He tries to keep the tempo moving because Bird gets into a rhythm. Qatato's been doing this for about five years, during which time he's had thousands of "assists," Qatato to Bird.

Bird likes to take his pregame shoot-around when it's quiet and he can concentrate completely on his technique, "so my teammates will have confidence going to me late in the game." Dressed in street clothes, he begins before the press gates officially open (5:30 on weeknights), though there are sometimes media people standing around. His most interested spectators are the security guards, who sit in a group watching him.

Sometimes Bird shoots only a few baskets; sometimes he'll shoot for twenty minutes or longer. Qatato says he can't tell from the number of shots Bird makes how he'll do in a game. He sometimes hits twenty jump-shots in a row, moving quickly in a semicircle. It's hypnotic to watch.

At 6:00, Bird gets a massage, then gets taped and dressed for the game.

Two hours before game time the opponents' bus arrives in front of the Garden. The players get off and walk together into their locker room.

Before the game, team doctor Arnold Scheller chats with the players in the trainer's room.

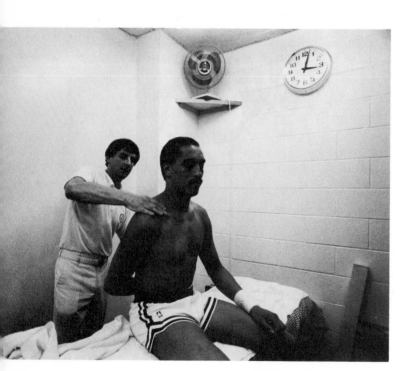

Massage therapist Vladimir Shulman works on DJ.

The Celtics coach arrives about two and a half hours before the game. His assistants and the other players arrive soon after. Most are dressed casually but neatly. Robert Parish is the dandy. He wears tailored business suits, dress shirts, and ties. Each player has his own routine. Each sees the trainer, stretches, shoots warm-ups, gets taped. The starters, and most others, get massages lasting five or ten minutes. The Celtics have their own massage therapist, Vladimir Shulman, a Russian expatriate who was once coach of the girls' handball team at Leningrad Olympic Reserve School.

Players generally don't eat for two hours before a game. If they do, they eat light food and drink orange juice from the locker-room ice chests. While some players warm up on the court, others watch videos of their opponents' last game, chat, or read their fan mail, which is delivered from the team office in bundles. Sometimes they autograph basketballs, which are given away to charity. The atmosphere is very relaxed and friendly.

Reporters come and go. The radio colorman, Glenn Ordway, arrives at 5:00 for a 7:30 game, going to the Celtics office to do a pregame interview with General Manager Jan Volk. Announcer Johnny Most, a thirty-year veteran who is a basketball institution in his own right, arrives at 6:00 to interview a player.

About an hour before game time, assistant coach Jimmy Rodgers begins diagraming the opponents' offense. The team meeting begins half an hour later and is closed to the press. K. C. Jones speaks first, briefly, then hands the discussion over to his assistants, who talk in turn about strategy. The players offer a comment or two. The same routine is followed at halftime.

The team then goes to the court for more warm-up shooting and stretching. The crowd has been filing in for an hour.

The game itself seems faster and rougher up close than when seen on television. Passes seem harder. The Celtics run many set plays, but the impression, up close, is of chaos. Everything happens quickly, flashing by. You can hear the players shouting to each other, calling out their plays or their opponents' plays or just yelling each others' names, hollering "Come here" or "Back up." When a player is knocked down, it sounds louder than on television. It seems like a playground game, but played faster, harder, better.

The ball boys also get in on the action. They hand out cups of water during time-outs, chase subs to pick up discarded warm-up clothes, dispense towels, put warm-up jackets over shoulders. One ball boy at each end wipes up sweat if a player falls.

At halftime the players retreat to the locker room for a ten-minute rest. They eat orange slices and drink water. A coach speaks to individual players about an assignment or a situation in the game. K. C. Jones addresses the whole team briefly. Some players do stretching exercises. Most just rest. They don't change uniforms or shower.

After halftime the fans press close to the court with their cameras. Ushers and security guards keep shooing them away, but they keep pressing in, leaning over, touching the players, asking for pictures. The players ignore them but the fans continue to prod them as if they were zoo exhibits.

After the game the players return to the trainer, and sometimes the masseur, to work on specific ailments. The media often go directly into the trainer's room after talking to the opponents' coach outside his dressing room. The press area is located behind the grandstand. It has a dining room where reporters eat for free before games. There's also a separate room with phone jacks for portable computers.

At weeknight games, reporters have to write stories in less than an hour in order to get them into the next morning's paper. Often they're finishing at courtside as the crowd is leaving. Fans watch in fascination as writers compose on their computer screens, summarizing a game that ended only minutes earlier. The reporter dials a number connecting him or her to the paper, presses some buttons on the computer, and the story is transmit-

The players get last-minute instructions from the coach.

ted. The reporter then goes into the locker room to get quotes to add to another story that will accompany the story about the game.

After showering and dressing, the players walk across the second-floor passageway to the storage area where their cars are parked. A young man who keeps the keys in a valet's cabinet retrieves the cars.

Autograph seekers gather at the bottom of the ramp. Many are regulars. Often there's a traffic jam as players and coaches drive down the ramp. The autograph seekers sometimes get bolder and come right up the ramp to the second-floor entrance.

John Murphy, a senior at Chelmsford High and an avid autograph seeker, says the Celtics used to walk with their wives down the ramp to get their cars. But they stopped doing that because of the crowds. He says most Celtics have more than one car. Many favor Jeep Cherokees. Dennis Johnson has a BMW, Danny Ainge a Mercedes and a Jeep, Larry Bird a white Lincoln Continental, K. C. Jones a Toyota.

"Sometimes Larry Bird sneaks out," Murphy says. "We don't know where. Someone says he goes out a side door. Parish tried to sneak out a side door on us tonight. But we caught him."

As the players file onto the court, the fans reach out to them.

Small fans snap pictures of tall players, as the Celtics take pregame drills. The game is about to begin.

Danny Ainge plays a tight
defense.

Fans live and die with their team.

**When a player returns to
the bench, a warmup
jacket is always waiting.**

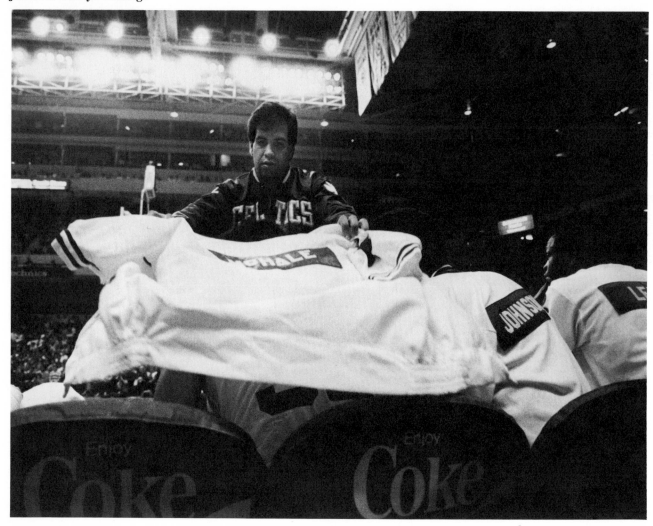

**Dennis Johnson re-enters
the game.**

Robert Parish hits the floor.

Radio announcer Johnny Most has a bird's-eye view of the court . . . while photographers shoot at courtside.

Reporters finish their game stories, then hurry to the locker room for postgame interviews.